PYTHON KICK START

FOR COMPLETE BEGINNERS

AVIRAL ASTHANA

ISBN 979-888606268-7

Dedicated to our respected professor "Pravin Panwar Sir"

Contents

Foreword

I am very happy to know not only because Aviral has been true friend and colleague of mine for more than twelve years, but also because he has become a good Author.

I want to convey this message from my small intro to the youth of the country that they should not only learn something from this book, but they should also learn a lot from Aviral's life because Aviral is a very hard working and simple man and nowadays he is also a successful business personality.

In Aviral, there is a lot of fame for discovering new things in this age, he has also achieved many successes now only. He has always been very helpful and generous to all, especially for poor and needy people, he is always standing first.

The most amazing thing about Aviral is that he has a strong attachment with animals and stray dogs. He has also opened a dog care foundation named "Avika Foundation" to help dogs and Animals. In that foundation, he feeds over a hundred stray dogs every week.

As a person and a friend, I have never found another guy like him. After seeing every work or proposals, he always says that it can happen, I have never heard from his mouth that it cannot happen. Aviral always says that there is always unique quality in every human being that is, he/she can do every work, the funda is to not delay. He does all his work very fast like he has 100 hands.

As far as I know Aviral, he works at least eighteen hours a day without any break. Aviral doesn't like to sit free, so maybe he is a moderate person.

Some people also named him "Mr. Cover" because he always covers his friend's mistakes by explaining them the right way like a mother is explaning to her childrens instead of bashing them.

Aviral says no one's wants to do mistake on his own free will, so if we will treat everyone with love instead of rebuking them, their morale will not be down and they will think many times before making any further mistake.

Apart from good quality of leadership, he also has a lot of good skills. He is also a very good person, he has knowledge of more than 18 programming languages and more than 7 states of local languages, which is very incredible for anyone.

One good thing about Aviral is also that, he is a very amazing culinary. He loves to cook for his family and friends.

He also loves gardening and planting trees. Aviral has also planted many trees in our college campus. He is a gem personality of this era.

Aviral says that the real man is that, who stay at only one girl through entire life. According to Aviral, every man should focus on one girl for entire life and stay with her only.

The problems come in our life and goes, only we have to find solution of that. Solution is not to leave anyone. According to him, he wants to erase breakup word from world that no one can leave anyone. With this thinking and hope, he is still waiting for one girl who has diched him and says that if she will not come back in his life, he says he will continue waiting rest of his life for her. We all friends explain a lot to him but he is not ready to accept that the girl has gone from his life.

I salute his thinking and pray to God that he should get that girl back very soon in his life. This quality of Aviral should also be learned by all of us.

Lots of congratulations to him for "Python Kick Start", we hope that as his life, this book will also be learnful & inspiring and will definetely inspire someone.

I want to tell the readers of this book that you will definitely learn something new from this book and it will also prevent the injustice being done in your or your society.

I assure you that this book will not only be interesting but will also be life-changing. I assure you that you will not regret this purchase.

At last again I heartily congratulate Aviral on his forthcoming book "Python Kick Start". I wish him all the best for his life that I pray to God for his good health and success at every step of his life. I am very blessed to have a true friend like him.

Love You Aviral.

Shailjakant Shukla
Author's Friend

Preface

This book is totally designed for beginners. This book contains all basic to advanced python exercises, projects and practise sets. There are lots of books in the market, but the simplicity of this book makes it unique. If you have to teach anyone related coding or anything, you have to make it more easier, so the learner can't face any problem. In this book we have started from basic along with what is python, History of Python and how Python is important nowadays for every coders. We have also tried to explain that the Python is very easy to code. By this book, every beginner can start coding in Python. The Author's tried his best to cover all important topic of Python in this Book. You can definitely enchance you coding skill at the end of this book. There are many Mini Projects also in this book like, How to make a calculator, Make a Dise Rolling Game, Any number to guess randomly, to print a song 99 times, or to guess aumber game, Fortune Telling Game, Random Password Generator & many more. In this Book Author's have presented you some unique Python programs to learn from basic.

Acknowledgements

Thank You, dear reader, for picking my book "Python Kick Start" which is completely for beginners and passionate developers.

For the very first, I would like to thank God for giving me such a amazing parents, who has always supported me in every situation when I needed. I am so blessed to have such good parents like them, who taught me to respect girls, discipline, manners, love for animals and the very special thing, how to live life.

Especially I would like to thank my dearest siblings (Abhibhaw Kumar Asthana & Ananya Asthana), without them I am nothing.

I would also like to thank all that people who inspired me at various stages of life.

The biggest thing of the family is its unity and love between every Members and my unity is my family. Thanks to all family members.

Some of my cousins who helped me at various stages of my life – Aaradhya, Aman, Ambuj, Anjali & my dearest Mayank.

Friends who have always supported me at every situation (Akash Tripathi, Mohit Kumar Prajapati, Utkarsh Dubey, Kartik, Manish, Abhishek, Vaibhav, Shashikant, Shailjakant, Manujendra, Sneha and my all dearest friends) & makes my life worth while. True friendship needs no description.

I am truly thankful to some of my college professors, Laxmi Shanker Sir, Arpit Chhabra Sir, Priyank Sirohi Sir, Pravin Panwar Sir, Manav Bansal Sir, Swati Singh ma'am, Sikha Agarwal ma'am & Nidhi Chauhan ma'am.

At the last but not the least, My Superhero – My Father, who always saves me when my mom use to talk after seeing my marksheets at school time “ki ye nhi kuch karega” that time my Superhero supports me.

Thank You Papa -

Prologue

This book is totally designed for beginners & it contains all basic to advanced python exercises along with some questions and answers, projects and practise sets. In this book we have started from basic python along with what is python, History of Python and how Python is important nowadays for every coders. We have also tried to explain that the Python is very easy to code. By this book, every beginner can start coding in Python. The Author's tried his best to cover all important topic of Python in this Book.

Complete Python soon in Volume 2 (Python Zero to Hero) from basic to advanced level.

Author's & Contributor's:

Author:

Aviral Asthana
(B.Tech)

Co-Author's:

Manujendra Singh (B.Tech)
Shailjakant Shukla (B.Tech)

Mail us: - author.aviral@gmail.com

CHAPTER ONE

Python Theory

Python is a general-purpose, interpreted, dynamic, object-oriented, high-level programming language. It is known as object-oriented because of its approach to developing applications.

Python is simple, easy, and provides high-level data structures. It is easy to learn and easy to modify as compare to others. Python has a huge community across the world, which makes coding easy.

The most impressive thing in python is, there is no compilation step in python. Python supports multiple programming patterns, including object-oriented, imperative, and functional or procedural programming styles. As compared to other languages, programmers fall in love with Python because of the increased productivity it provides, as I mentioned above there is no compilation step in python, so the debug step is much fast, this is also a thing which programmers love most in this language.

There are also more than 137000 libraries present of python, which plays a major role while developing and also makes coding easy. The most amazing thing about Python libraries is, they are free and open to use. It is an open-source language that means anyone can download, install and code it free.

History of Python

It was initially designed by Guido van Rossum in 1991 and developed by Python Software Foundation. It was mainly developed for emphasis on code readability, and its syntax allows programmers to express concepts in fewer lines of code.

In the late 1980s, history was about to be written. It was that time when working on Python started. Soon after that, Guido Van Rossum began doing its application based work in December of 1989 by at Centrum Wiskunde & Informatica (CWI) which is situated in Netherland. It was started firstly as a hobby project because he was looking for an interesting project to keep him occupied during Christmas. The programming language which Python is said to have succeeded is ABC Programming Language, which had the interfacing with the Amoeba Operating System and had the feature of exception handling. He had already helped to create ABC earlier in his career and he had seen some issues with ABC but liked most of the features. After that what he did as really very clever. He had taken the syntax of ABC, and some of its good features. It came with a lot of complaints too, so he fixed those issues completely and had created a good scripting language which had removed all the flaws. The inspiration for the name came from BBC's TV Show – 'Monty Python's Flying Circus', as he was a big fan of the TV show and also he wanted a short, unique and slightly mysterious name for his invention and hence he named it Python! He was the "Benevolent dictator for life" (BDFL) until he stepped down from the position as the leader on 12th July 2018. For quite some time he used to work for Google, but currently, he is working at Dropbox.

The language was finally released in 1991. When it was released, it used a lot fewer codes to express the concepts, when we compare it with Java, C++ & C. Its design philosophy was quite good too. Its main objective is to provide code readability and advanced developer productivity. When it was released it had more than enough capability to provide classes with inheritance, several core data types exception handling and functions.

When i was writing this Book, the latest version of Python was - Python 3.9.6

There are many languages but Why Python ?

- Easy to Code
- Open Source and Free
- Support for GUI
- Object Oriented Approach
- High Level Language
- Integrated by Nature
- Highly Portable
- Highly Dynamic
- Extensive Array of Library
- Support for other Languages
- It's easy to learn – the time needed to learn Python is shorter than for many other languages; this means that it's possible to start the actual programming faster;
- It's easy to teach – the teaching workload is smaller than that needed by other languages; this means that the teacher can put more emphasis on general (language-independent) programming techniques, not wasting energy on exotic tricks, strange exceptions and

incomprehensible rules;

- It's easy to use for writing new software – it's often possible to write code faster when using Python;
- It's easy to understand – it's also often easier to understand someone else's code faster if it is written in Python;
- It's easy to obtain, install and deploy – Python is free, open and multiplatform; not all languages can boast that.

Advantages of Python

- Presence of third-party modules.
- Extensive support libraries(NumPy for numerical calculations, Pandas for data analytics etc).
- Open source and community development.
- Versatile, Easy to read, learn and write.
- User-friendly data structures.
- High-level language.
- Dynamically typed language(No need to mention data type based on the value assigned, it takes data type).
- Object-oriented language.
- Portable and Interactive.
- Ideal for prototypes – provide more functionality with less coding.
- Highly Efficient(Python's clean object-oriented design provides enhanced process control, and the language is equipped with excellent text processing and integration capabilities, as well as its own unit testing framework, which makes it more efficient).
- (IoT)Internet of Things Opportunities.
- Interpreted Language.

- Portable across Operating systems.

Python used in Application

- GUI based desktop applications.
- Graphic design, image processing applications, Games, and Scientific/ computational Applications.
- Web frameworks and applications.
- Enterprise and Business applications.
- Operating Systems.
- Education.
- Database Access.
- Language Development.
- Prototyping.
- Software Development.

Uses of Python

- Python can serve as a scripting language for web applications, e.g., via mod wsgi for the Apache web server.
- Web frameworks like Django, Pylons, Pyramid, TurboGears, web2py, Tornado, Flask, Bottle and Zope support developers in the design and maintenance of complex applications.
- Libraries such as NumPy, SciPy and Matplotlib allow the effective use of Python in scientific computing, with specialized libraries such as Biopython and Astropy providing domain-specific functionality.

- Python is commonly used in artificial intelligence projects and machine learning projects with the help of libraries like TensorFlow, Keras, Pytorch and Scikit-learn.
- Python has been successfully embedded in many software products as a scripting language, including in finite element method software such as Abaqus, 3D parametric modeler like FreeCAD, 3D animation packages such as 3ds Max, Blender, Cinema 4D, etc.

CHAPTER TWO

Python Begins Basic

"Only your skills will help you to get success in your life; because your degree is just a statement of your cram.

Aviral Kumar -"

Starting Python Code from the slight beginning:

1: Program to print 'Hello'.

<u>Python Code:</u>

```
print("Hello")
```

<u>Output:</u>

```
Hello
```

2: Program to print following string in below specific format.

Humpty Dumpty sat on a wall, Humpty Dumpty had a great fall, All the king's horses and all the King's men, Couldn't put Humpty Dumpty together again.

Specific Format:

Humpty Dumpty sat on a wall,
Humpty Dumpty had a great fall,
All the king's horses and all the King's men,
Couldn't put Humpty Dumpty together again.

Python Code:

```
print("Humpty Dumpty sat on a wall, \n\tHumpty Dumpty had a great fall \n\t\tAll the king's horses and all the King's men, \n\t\tCouldn't put Humpty Dumpty together again.")
```

Output:

Humpty Dumpty sat on a wall,
Humpty Dumpty had a great fall,
All the king's horses and all the King's men,
Couldn't put Humpty Dumpty together again.

3: Program to add two numbers.

Python Code:

```
x = 5
y = 10
print(x + y)
```

Output:

15

4: Program to add two numbers with user input.

Python Code:

```
x = input("Type a number: ")
y = input("Type another number: ")
sum = int(x) + int(y)
print("The sum is: ", sum)
```

Output:

Type a number:

Type another number:

5: Program to add two numbers with message.

Python Code:

```
num1 = 1.5
num2 = 6.3 # Now add two numbers
sum = num1 + num2 # Now display the sum
print('The sum of {0} and {1} is {2}'.format(num1, num2, sum))
```

Output:

The sum of 1.5 and 6.3 is 7.8

6: Program to display calendar

Python Code:

```
import calendar
# Enter the month and year
yy = int(input("Enter year: "))
mm = int(input("Enter month: "))
# display the calendar
print(calendar.month(yy,mm))
```

Output:

The output will be display calender with date, day, month and year.

7: Program to Check Prime Number

Python Code:

```
# A default function for Prime checking conditions
def PrimeChecker(a):
# Checking that given number is more than 1
if a > 1:
# Iterating over the given number with for loop
for j in range(2, int(a/2) + 1):
# If the given number is divisible or not
if (a % j) == 0:
print(a, "is not a prime number")
break
# Else it is a prime number
else:
```

```
print(a, "is a prime number")
# If the given number is 1
else:
print(a, "is not a prime number")
# Taking an input number from the user
a = int(input("Enter an input number:"))
# Printing result
PrimeChecker(a)
```

Output:

Enter an input number:17

17 is a prime number

8: Program to Find the Factorial of a Number.

Python Code:

```
num = int(input("Enter a number: "))
factorial = 1
if num < 0:
print(" Factorial does not exist for negative numbers")
elif num == 0:
print("The factorial of 0 is 1")
else:
for i in range(1,num + 1):
factorial = factorial*i
print("The factorial of",num,"is",factorial)
```

Output:

Enter a number: 10

The factorial of 10 is 3628800

9: Program to Print the Fibonacci sequence.

Python Code:

```
n_terms = int(input ("How many terms the user wants to print? "))
# First two terms
n_1 = 0
n_2 = 1
count = 0
# Now, we will check if the number of terms is valid or not
if n_terms <= 0:
print ("Please enter a positive integer, the given number is not valid")
# if there is only one term, it will return n_1
elif n_terms == 1:
print ("The Fibonacci sequence of the numbers up to", n_terms, ": ")
print(n_1)
# Then we will generate Fibonacci sequence of number
else:
print ("The fibonacci sequence of the numbers is:")
while count < n_terms:
print(n_1)
nth = n_1 + n_2
# At last, we will update values
n_1 = n_2
n_2 = nth
count += 1
```

Output:

How many terms the user wants to print? 13
The Fibonacci sequence of the numbers is:
0
1
1
2
3
5
8
13
21
34
55
89
144

10: Program to Find the Sum of Natural Numbers.

Python Code:

```
num = int(input("Enter a number: "))
if num < 0:
print("Enter a positive number")
else:
sum = 0
# use while loop to iterate un till zero
while(num > 0):
sum += num
num -= 1
```

```
print("The sum is",sum)
```

Output:

If you have entered 100 (exp.)

The sum is 5050

11: Program to Find LCM.

Python Code:

```
# defining a function to calculate LCM
def calculate_lcm(x, y):
# selecting the greater number
if x > y:
greater = x
else:
greater = y
while(True):
if((greater % x == 0) and (greater % y == 0)):
lcm = greater
break
greater += 1
return lcm
# taking input from users
num1 = int(input("Enter first number: "))
num2 = int(input("Enter second number: "))
# printing the result for the users
print("The L.C.M. of", num1,"and", num2,"is", calculate_lcm(num1, num2))
```

Output:

Enter first number: 3
Enter second number: 4
The L.C.M. of 3 and 4 is 12

12: Program to Find HCF.

Python Code:

```
# defining a function to calculate HCF
def calculate_hcf(x, y):
# selecting the smaller number
if x > y:
smaller = y
else:
smaller = x
for i in range(1,smaller + 1):
if((x % i == 0) and (y % i == 0)):
hcf = i
return hcf
# taking input from users
num1 = int(input("Enter first number: "))
num2 = int(input("Enter second number: "))
# printing the result for the users
print("The H.C.F. of", num1,"and", num2,"is", calculate_hcf(num1, num2))
```

Output:

Enter first number: 8
Enter second number: 12
The H.C.F. of 8 and 12 is 4

13: Program to Display Fibonacci Sequence Using Recursion.

Python Code:

```
def recur_fibo(n):
if n <= 1:
return n
else:
return(recur_fibo(n-1) + recur_fibo(n-2))
# take input from the user
nterms = int(input("How many terms? "))
# check if the number of terms is valid
if nterms <= 0:
print("Plese enter a positive integer")
else:
print("Fibonacci sequence:")
for i in range(nterms):
print(recur_fibo(i))
```

Output:

```
Febonacci Sequence:
0
1
1
2
3
5
8
13
21
```

34
55
89

14: Program to Find Factorial of Number Using Recursion.

Python Code:

```
def recur_factorial(n):
if n == 1:
return n
else:
return n*recur_factorial(n-1)
# take input from the user
num = int(input("Enter a number: "))
# check is the number is negative
if num < 0:
print("Sorry, factorial does not exist for negative numbers")
elif num == 0:
print("The factorial of 0 is 1")
else:
print("The factorial of",num,"is",recur_factorial(num))
```

Output:

Sorry, factorial does not exist for negative numbers

15: Program to check if the given number is Happy Number.

Python Code:

```
#isHappyNumber() will determine whether a number is happy or not
def isHappyNumber(num):
rem = sum = 0;
#Calculates the sum of squares of digits
while(num > 0):
rem = num%10;
sum = sum + (rem*rem);
num = num//10;
return sum;
num = 82;
result = num;
while(result != 1 and result != 4):
result = isHappyNumber(result);
#Happy number always ends with 1
if(result == 1):
print(str(num) + " is a happy number");
#Unhappy number ends in a cycle of repeating numbers which contain 4
elif(result == 4):
print(str(num) + " is not a happy number");
```

Output:

82 is a happy number

16: Program to print all happy numbers between 1 and 100.

Python Code:

```
#isHappyNumber() will determine whether a number is happy or not
def isHappyNumber(num):
rem = sum = 0;
#Calculates the sum of squares of digits
while(num > 0):
rem = num%10;
sum = sum + (rem*rem);
num = num//10;
return sum;
#Displays all happy numbers between 1 and 100
print("List of happy numbers between 1 and 100: ");
for i in range(1, 101):
result = i;
#Happy number always ends with 1 and
#unhappy number ends in a cycle of repeating numbers which contains 4
while(result != 1 and result != 4):
result = isHappyNumber(result);
if(result == 1):
print(i),
print(" "),
```

Output:

List of happy numbers between 1 and 100:
1 7 10 13 19 23 28 31 32 44 49 68 70 79 82 86 91 94 97 100

17: Program to print all pronic numbers between 1 and 100.

Python Code:

```
#isPronicNumber() will determine whether a given number is a pronic number or not
def isPronicNumber(num):
flag = False;
for j in range(1, num+1):
#Checks for pronic number by multiplying consecutive numbers
if((j*(j+1)) == num):
flag = True;
break;
return flag;
#Displays pronic numbers between 1 and 100
print("Pronic numbers between 1 and 100: ");
for i in range(1, 101):
if(isPronicNumber(i)):
print(i),
print(" "),
```

Output:

Pronic numbers between 1 and 100:
2 6 12 20 30 42 56 72 90

18: Program to print the largest element in an array.

Python Code:

```
#Initialize array
arr = [25, 11, 7, 75, 56];
#Initialize max with first element of array.
max = arr[0];
#Loop through the array
for i in range(0, len(arr)):
#Compare elements of array with max
if(arr[i] > max):
max = arr[i];
print("Largest element present in given array: " + str(max));
```

Output:

Largest element present in given array: 75

19: Program to print the elements of an array.

Python Code:

```
#Initialize array
arr = [1, 2, 3, 4, 5];
print("Elements of given array: ");
#Loop through the array by incrementing the value of i
for i in range(0, len(arr)):
print(arr[i]),
```

Output:

Elements of given array:

1 2 3 4 5

20: Program to right rotate the elements of an array.

Python Code:

```
#Initialize array
arr = [1, 2, 3, 4, 5];
#n determine the number of times an array should be rotated
n = 3;
#Displays original array
print("Original array: ");
for i in range(0, len(arr)):
print(arr[i]),
#Rotate the given array by n times toward right
for i in range(0, n):
#Stores the last element of array
last = arr[len(arr)-1];
for j in range(len(arr)-1, -1, -1):
#Shift element of array by one
arr[j] = arr[j-1];
#Last element of the array will be added to the start of the array.
arr[0] = last;
print();
#Displays resulting array after rotation
print("Array after right rotation: ");
```

```
for i in range(0, len(arr)):
print(arr[i]),
```

Output:

Original Array:

1 2 3 4 5

Array after right rotation:

3 4 5 1 2

21: Program to Add Two Matrices

Python Code:

```
X = [[1,2,3],
[4,5,6],
[7,8,9]]

Y = [[10,11,12],
[13,14,15],
[16,17,18]]

Result = [[0,0,0],
[0,0,0],
[0,0,0]]
# iterate through rows
for i in range(len(X)):
# iterate through columns
for j in range(len(X[0])):
result[i][j] = X[i][j] + Y[i][j]
for r in result:
print(r)
```

Output:

[11, 13, 15]
[17, 19, 21]
[23, 25, 27]

22: Program to Multiply Two Matrices.

Python Code:

```
Define two matrix A and B in program
A = [[5, 4, 3],
[2, 4, 6],
[4, 7, 9]]
B = [[3, 2, 4],
[4, 3, 6],
[2, 7, 5]]
# Define an empty matrix to store multiplication result
multiResult = [[0, 0, 0],
[0, 0, 0],
[0, 0, 0]]
# Using nested for loop method on A & B matrix
for m in range(len(A)):
for n in range(len(B[0])):
for o in range(len(B)):
multiResult[m][n] += A[m][o] * B[o][n] # Storing multiplication result in empty matrix
# Printing multiplication result in the output
print("The multiplication result of matrix A and B is: ")
for res in multiResult:
print(res)
```

Output:

The multiplication result of matrix A and B is:

[37, 43, 59]

[34, 58, 62]

[58, 92, 103]

23: Program to Transpose a Matrix.

Python Code:

```
# Define a matrix A
A = [[5, 4, 3],
[2, 4, 6],
[4, 7, 9],
[8, 1, 3]]
# Define an empty matrix of reverse order
transResult = [[0, 0, 0, 0],
[0, 0, 0, 0],
[0, 0, 0, 0]]
# Use nested for loop on matrix A
for a in range(len(A)):
for b in range(len(A[0])):
transResult[b][a] = A[a][b] # store transpose result on empty matrix
# Printing result in the output
print("The transpose of matrix A is: ")
for res in transResult:
print(res)
```

Output:

The transpose of matrix A is:

[5, 2, 4, 8]
[4, 4, 7, 1]
[3, 6, 9, 3]

24: Reverse a string in Python.

Python Code:

```
def reverse_string(str):
str1 = "" # Declaring empty string to store the reversed string
for i in str:
str1 = i + str1
return str1 # It will return the reverse string to the caller function
str = "JavaTpoint" # Given String
print("The original string is: ",str)
print("The reverse string is",reverse_string(str)) # Function call
```

Output:

('The original string is: ', 'JavaTpoint')
('The reverse string is', 'tniopTavaJ')

25: Program to solve quadratic equation.

Python Code:

```
# import complex math module
```

```
import cmath
a = float(input(‘Enter a: ’))
b = float(input(‘Enter b: ’))
c = float(input(‘Enter c: ’))
# calculate the discriminant
d = (b**2) - (4*a*c)
# find two solutions
sol1 = (-b-cmath.sqrt(d))/(2*a)
sol2 = (-b+cmath.sqrt(d))/(2*a)
print(‘The solution are {0} and {1}’.format(sol1,sol2))
```

Output:

Enter a: 8

Enter b: 5

Enter c: 9

The solution are (-0.3125-1.0135796712641785j) and (-0.3125+1.0135796712641785j)

Python Shorts

1. What are the key features of Python?

Ans: The Answer is -

- Easy to code.
- Python is a high-level programming language.
- Free and Open Source.
- Object-Oriented Language.
- GUI Programming Support.
- High-Level Language.
- Extensible feature.
- Python is Portable language.
- Python is Integrated language.

2. What type of language is python? Programming or scripting?

Ans: Python is capable of scripting, but in general sense, it is considered as a general-purpose programming language.

3. Explain decorators in Python?

Ans: Decorators are used to add some design patterns to a function without changing its structure. Decorators generally are defined before the function they are enhancing. To apply a decorator we first define the decorator function.

4. What are the common built-in data types in Python?

Ans: The Answer is -

- Numbers
- String

- Tuples
- Dictionaries
- String
- Boolean
- Set

5. Explain slicing in Python?

Ans: Slicing is used to access parts of sequences like lists, tuples, and strings.

6. What are Keywords in Python?

Ans: Keywords in python are reserved words that have special meaning. They are generally used to define type of variables.

7. How many keywords are there in Python?

Ans: There are 33 Keywords in Python -

- And
- Or
- Not
- If
- Elif
- Else
- For
- While
- Break
- As
- Def
- Lambda
- Pass
- Return
- True
- False
- Try

- With
- Assert
- Class
- Continue
- Del
- Except
- Finally
- From
- Global
- Import
- In
- Is
- None
- Nonlocal
- Raise
- Yield

8. Explain namespace in Python?

Ans: A namespace is a naming system used to make sure that names are unique to avoid naming conflicts.

9. What is local variable in Python?

Ans: Any variable declared inside a function is known as a local variable. This variable is present in the local space and not in the global space.

10. What is Global Variable in Python?

Ans: Variables declared outside a function or in global space are called global variables. These variables can be accessed by any function in the program.

11. What is type conversion in Python?

Ans: The Answer is -

- int()
- float()

- ord()
- hex()
- oct()
- tuple()
- set()
- list()
- dict()
- str()

12. Difference between Python Arrays and lists?

Ans: Arrays and lists, in Python, have the same way of storing data. But, arrays can hold only a single data type elements whereas lists can hold any data type elements.

13. What are functions in Python?

Ans: A function is a block of code which is executed only when it is called. To define a Python function, the def keyword is used.

14. What is self in Python?

Ans: Self is an instance or an object of a class.

15. What are python iterators?

Ans: Iterators are objects which can be traversed though or iterated upon.

16. How to write comments in python?

Ans: You can write Comments in Python using a # character.

17. What are the generators in python?

Ans: Functions that return an iterable set of items are called generators.

18. What is pickling inPython?

Ans: Pickle module accepts any Python object and converts it into a string representation and dumps it into a file by using dump function, this process is called pickling

19. What is unpickling in Python?

Ans: While the process of retrieving original Python objects from the stored string representation is called unpickling.

20. What are docstrings in Python?

Ans: Docstrings are not actually comments.

21. What is a dictionary in Python?

Ans: The built-in datatypes in Python is called dictionary.

22. What are Python packages?

Ans: Python packages are namespaces containing multiple modules.

23.What are Python libraries?

Ans: Python libraries are a collection of Python packages.

24. What is split used for?

Ans: The split() method is used to separate a given string in Python.

25. How to import modules in python?

Ans: Modules can be imported using the import keyword.

Mini Projects

Here are some selected Mini Projects:

Project - 1:

Create a Python project to guess a number that has randomly selected.

Python Code:

```
import random
number=random.randrange(0,100)
guessCheck="wrong"
print("Welcome to Number Guess")
while guessCheck=="wrong":
response=int(input("Please input a number between 0 and 100:"))
try:
val=int(response)
except ValueError:
print("This is not a valid integer. Please try again")
continue
val=int (response)
if val<number:
print("This is lower than actual number. Please try again.")
```

```
elif val>number:
print("This is higher than actual number. Please try again.")
else:
print("This is the correct number")
guessCheck="correct"
print("Thank you for playing Number Guess of Aviral. See you again, Take Care")
```

Output:

- Welcome to Number Guess
- Please input a number between 0 and 100:

(suppose i enter 31, then the output will be)

- This is higher than actual number. Please try again.
- Please input a number between 0 and 100:

(Now i will enter 9, then the output will be)

- This is the correct number
- Thank you for playing Number Guess. See you again

Project - 2:

Create a Python project that prints out every line of the song "99 bottles of beer on the wall."

Note: *Try to use a built in function instead of manually type all the lines.*

Python Code:

```
def sing(n):
if (n == 1):
objects = ‘bottle’
objectsMinusOne = ‘bottles’
elif (n == 2):
objects = ‘bottles’
objectsMinusOne = ‘bottle’
else:
objects = ‘bottles’
objectsMinusOne = ‘bottles’
if (n > 0):
print(str(n) + " " + objects + " of beer on the wall, " + str(n) + " " + objects + " of beer.")
print("Take one down and pass it around, " + str(n-1) + " " + objectsMinusOne + " of beer on the wall.")
print(" ")
elif (n == 0):
print("No more bottles of beer on the wall, no more bottles of beer.")
print("Go to the store and buy some more, 99 bottles of beer on the wall.")
else:
print("Error: Wheres the booze?")
bottles = 99
while bottles >= 0:
sing(bottles)
bottles -= 1
```

Output:

- 99 bottles of beer on the wall, 99 bottles of beer.
- Take one down and pass it around, 98 bottles of beer on the wall.
-
- 98 bottles of beer on the wall, 98 bottles of beer.
- Take one down and pass it around, 97 bottles of beer on the wall.
-
- 97 bottles of beer on the wall, 97 bottles of beer.
- Take one down and pass it around, 96 bottles of beer on the wall.
-
- 96 bottles of beer on the wall, 96 bottles of beer.
- Take one down and pass it around, 95 bottles of beer on the wall.
-
- 95 bottles of beer on the wall, 95 bottles of beer.
- Take one down and pass it around, 94 bottles of beer on the wall.
-
- 94 bottles of beer on the wall, 94 bottles of beer.
- Take one down and pass it around, 93 bottles of beer on the wall.
-
- 93 bottles of beer on the wall, 93 bottles of beer.
- Take one down and pass it around, 92 bottles of beer on the wall.
-
- 92 bottles of beer on the wall, 92 bottles of beer.
- Take one down and pass it around, 91 bottles of beer on the wall.
-

- 91 bottles of beer on the wall, 91 bottles of beer.
- Take one down and pass it around, 90 bottles of beer on the wall.
-
- 90 bottles of beer on the wall, 90 bottles of beer.
- Take one down and pass it around, 89 bottles of beer on the wall.
-
- 89 bottles of beer on the wall, 89 bottles of beer.
- Take one down and pass it around, 88 bottles of beer on the wall.
-
- 88 bottles of beer on the wall, 88 bottles of beer.
- Take one down and pass it around, 87 bottles of beer on the wall.
-
- 87 bottles of beer on the wall, 87 bottles of beer.
- Take one down and pass it around, 86 bottles of beer on the wall.
-
- 86 bottles of beer on the wall, 86 bottles of beer.
- Take one down and pass it around, 85 bottles of beer on the wall.
-
- 85 bottles of beer on the wall, 85 bottles of beer.
- Take one down and pass it around, 84 bottles of beer on the wall.
-
- 84 bottles of beer on the wall, 84 bottles of beer.
- Take one down and pass it around, 83 bottles of beer on the wall.
-
- 83 bottles of beer on the wall, 83 bottles of beer.

- Take one down and pass it around, 82 bottles of beer on the wall.
-
- 82 bottles of beer on the wall, 82 bottles of beer.
- Take one down and pass it around, 81 bottles of beer on the wall.
-
- 81 bottles of beer on the wall, 81 bottles of beer.
- Take one down and pass it around, 80 bottles of beer on the wall.
-
- 80 bottles of beer on the wall, 80 bottles of beer.
- Take one down and pass it around, 79 bottles of beer on the wall.
-
- 79 bottles of beer on the wall, 79 bottles of beer.
- Take one down and pass it around, 78 bottles of beer on the wall.
-
- 78 bottles of beer on the wall, 78 bottles of beer.
- Take one down and pass it around, 77 bottles of beer on the wall.
-
- 77 bottles of beer on the wall, 77 bottles of beer.
- Take one down and pass it around, 76 bottles of beer on the wall.
-
- 76 bottles of beer on the wall, 76 bottles of beer.
- Take one down and pass it around, 75 bottles of beer on the wall.
-
- 75 bottles of beer on the wall, 75 bottles of beer.
- Take one down and pass it around, 74 bottles of beer on

the wall.

-
- 74 bottles of beer on the wall, 74 bottles of beer.
- Take one down and pass it around, 73 bottles of beer on the wall.
-
- 73 bottles of beer on the wall, 73 bottles of beer.
- Take one down and pass it around, 72 bottles of beer on the wall.
-
- 72 bottles of beer on the wall, 72 bottles of beer.
- Take one down and pass it around, 71 bottles of beer on the wall.
-
- 71 bottles of beer on the wall, 71 bottles of beer.
- Take one down and pass it around, 70 bottles of beer on the wall.
-
- 70 bottles of beer on the wall, 70 bottles of beer.
- Take one down and pass it around, 69 bottles of beer on the wall.
-
- 69 bottles of beer on the wall, 69 bottles of beer.
- Take one down and pass it around, 68 bottles of beer on the wall.
-
- 68 bottles of beer on the wall, 68 bottles of beer.
- Take one down and pass it around, 67 bottles of beer on the wall.
-
- 67 bottles of beer on the wall, 67 bottles of beer.
- Take one down and pass it around, 66 bottles of beer on the wall.
-

- 66 bottles of beer on the wall, 66 bottles of beer.
- Take one down and pass it around, 65 bottles of beer on the wall.
-
- 65 bottles of beer on the wall, 65 bottles of beer.
- Take one down and pass it around, 64 bottles of beer on the wall.
-
- 64 bottles of beer on the wall, 64 bottles of beer.
- Take one down and pass it around, 63 bottles of beer on the wall.
-
- 63 bottles of beer on the wall, 63 bottles of beer.
- Take one down and pass it around, 62 bottles of beer on the wall.
-
- 62 bottles of beer on the wall, 62 bottles of beer.
- Take one down and pass it around, 61 bottles of beer on the wall.
-
- 61 bottles of beer on the wall, 61 bottles of beer.
- Take one down and pass it around, 60 bottles of beer on the wall.
-
- 60 bottles of beer on the wall, 60 bottles of beer.
- Take one down and pass it around, 59 bottles of beer on the wall.
-
- 59 bottles of beer on the wall, 59 bottles of beer.
- Take one down and pass it around, 58 bottles of beer on the wall.
-
- 58 bottles of beer on the wall, 58 bottles of beer.

- Take one down and pass it around, 57 bottles of beer on the wall.
-
- 57 bottles of beer on the wall, 57 bottles of beer.
- Take one down and pass it around, 56 bottles of beer on the wall.
-
- 56 bottles of beer on the wall, 56 bottles of beer.
- Take one down and pass it around, 55 bottles of beer on the wall.
-
- 55 bottles of beer on the wall, 55 bottles of beer.
- Take one down and pass it around, 54 bottles of beer on the wall.
-
- 54 bottles of beer on the wall, 54 bottles of beer.
- Take one down and pass it around, 53 bottles of beer on the wall.
-
- 53 bottles of beer on the wall, 53 bottles of beer.
- Take one down and pass it around, 52 bottles of beer on the wall.
-
- 52 bottles of beer on the wall, 52 bottles of beer.
- Take one down and pass it around, 51 bottles of beer on the wall.
-
- 51 bottles of beer on the wall, 51 bottles of beer.
- Take one down and pass it around, 50 bottles of beer on the wall.
-
- 50 bottles of beer on the wall, 50 bottles of beer.
- Take one down and pass it around, 49 bottles of beer on

the wall.

-
- 49 bottles of beer on the wall, 49 bottles of beer.
- Take one down and pass it around, 48 bottles of beer on the wall.
-
- 48 bottles of beer on the wall, 48 bottles of beer.
- Take one down and pass it around, 47 bottles of beer on the wall.
-
- 47 bottles of beer on the wall, 47 bottles of beer.
- Take one down and pass it around, 46 bottles of beer on the wall.
-
- 46 bottles of beer on the wall, 46 bottles of beer.
- Take one down and pass it around, 45 bottles of beer on the wall.
-
- 45 bottles of beer on the wall, 45 bottles of beer.
- Take one down and pass it around, 44 bottles of beer on the wall.
-
- 44 bottles of beer on the wall, 44 bottles of beer.
- Take one down and pass it around, 43 bottles of beer on the wall.
-
- 43 bottles of beer on the wall, 43 bottles of beer.
- Take one down and pass it around, 42 bottles of beer on the wall.
-
- 42 bottles of beer on the wall, 42 bottles of beer.
- Take one down and pass it around, 41 bottles of beer on the wall.
-

- 41 bottles of beer on the wall, 41 bottles of beer.
- Take one down and pass it around, 40 bottles of beer on the wall.
-
- 40 bottles of beer on the wall, 40 bottles of beer.
- Take one down and pass it around, 39 bottles of beer on the wall.
-
- 39 bottles of beer on the wall, 39 bottles of beer.
- Take one down and pass it around, 38 bottles of beer on the wall.
-
- 38 bottles of beer on the wall, 38 bottles of beer.
- Take one down and pass it around, 37 bottles of beer on the wall.
-
- 37 bottles of beer on the wall, 37 bottles of beer.
- Take one down and pass it around, 36 bottles of beer on the wall.
-
- 36 bottles of beer on the wall, 36 bottles of beer.
- Take one down and pass it around, 35 bottles of beer on the wall.
-
- 35 bottles of beer on the wall, 35 bottles of beer.
- Take one down and pass it around, 34 bottles of beer on the wall.
-
- 34 bottles of beer on the wall, 34 bottles of beer.
- Take one down and pass it around, 33 bottles of beer on the wall.
-
- 33 bottles of beer on the wall, 33 bottles of beer.

- Take one down and pass it around, 32 bottles of beer on the wall.
-
- 32 bottles of beer on the wall, 32 bottles of beer.
- Take one down and pass it around, 31 bottles of beer on the wall.
-
- 31 bottles of beer on the wall, 31 bottles of beer.
- Take one down and pass it around, 30 bottles of beer on the wall.
-
- 30 bottles of beer on the wall, 30 bottles of beer.
- Take one down and pass it around, 29 bottles of beer on the wall.
-
- 29 bottles of beer on the wall, 29 bottles of beer.
- Take one down and pass it around, 28 bottles of beer on the wall.
-
- 28 bottles of beer on the wall, 28 bottles of beer.
- Take one down and pass it around, 27 bottles of beer on the wall.
-
- 27 bottles of beer on the wall, 27 bottles of beer.
- Take one down and pass it around, 26 bottles of beer on the wall.
-
- 26 bottles of beer on the wall, 26 bottles of beer.
- Take one down and pass it around, 25 bottles of beer on the wall.
-
- 25 bottles of beer on the wall, 25 bottles of beer.
- Take one down and pass it around, 24 bottles of beer on

the wall.

-
- 24 bottles of beer on the wall, 24 bottles of beer.
- Take one down and pass it around, 23 bottles of beer on the wall.
-
- 23 bottles of beer on the wall, 23 bottles of beer.
- Take one down and pass it around, 22 bottles of beer on the wall.
-
- 22 bottles of beer on the wall, 22 bottles of beer.
- Take one down and pass it around, 21 bottles of beer on the wall.
-
- 21 bottles of beer on the wall, 21 bottles of beer.
- Take one down and pass it around, 20 bottles of beer on the wall.
-
- 20 bottles of beer on the wall, 20 bottles of beer.
- Take one down and pass it around, 19 bottles of beer on the wall.
-
- 19 bottles of beer on the wall, 19 bottles of beer.
- Take one down and pass it around, 18 bottles of beer on the wall.
-
- 18 bottles of beer on the wall, 18 bottles of beer.
- Take one down and pass it around, 17 bottles of beer on the wall.
-
- 17 bottles of beer on the wall, 17 bottles of beer.
- Take one down and pass it around, 16 bottles of beer on the wall.
-

- 16 bottles of beer on the wall, 16 bottles of beer.
- Take one down and pass it around, 15 bottles of beer on the wall.
-
- 15 bottles of beer on the wall, 15 bottles of beer.
- Take one down and pass it around, 14 bottles of beer on the wall.
-
- 14 bottles of beer on the wall, 14 bottles of beer.
- Take one down and pass it around, 13 bottles of beer on the wall.
-
- 13 bottles of beer on the wall, 13 bottles of beer.
- Take one down and pass it around, 12 bottles of beer on the wall.
-
- 12 bottles of beer on the wall, 12 bottles of beer.
- Take one down and pass it around, 11 bottles of beer on the wall.
-
- 11 bottles of beer on the wall, 11 bottles of beer.
- Take one down and pass it around, 10 bottles of beer on the wall.
-
- 10 bottles of beer on the wall, 10 bottles of beer.
- Take one down and pass it around, 9 bottles of beer on the wall.
-
- 9 bottles of beer on the wall, 9 bottles of beer.
- Take one down and pass it around, 8 bottles of beer on the wall.
-
- 8 bottles of beer on the wall, 8 bottles of beer.

- Take one down and pass it around, 7 bottles of beer on the wall.
-
- 7 bottles of beer on the wall, 7 bottles of beer.
- Take one down and pass it around, 6 bottles of beer on the wall.
-
- 6 bottles of beer on the wall, 6 bottles of beer.
- Take one down and pass it around, 5 bottles of beer on the wall.
-
- 5 bottles of beer on the wall, 5 bottles of beer.
- Take one down and pass it around, 4 bottles of beer on the wall.
-
- 4 bottles of beer on the wall, 4 bottles of beer.
- Take one down and pass it around, 3 bottles of beer on the wall.
-
- 3 bottles of beer on the wall, 3 bottles of beer.
- Take one down and pass it around, 2 bottles of beer on the wall.
-
- 2 bottles of beer on the wall, 2 bottles of beer.
- Take one down and pass it around, 1 bottle of beer on the wall.
-
- 1 bottle of beer on the wall, 1 bottle of beer.
- Take one down and pass it around, 0 bottles of beer on the wall.
-
- No more bottles of beer on the wall, no more bottles of beer.

- Go to the store and buy some more, 99 bottles of beer on the wall.

Project - 3:

Create a Python project of a Magic 8 Ball which is a toy used for fortune-telling or seeking advice.

Note :

- Allow the user to input their question.
- Show an in progress message.
- Create 10/20 responses, and show a random response.
- Allow the user to ask another question/advice or quit the game.

Python Code:

```
import random
answers = [‘It is certain’, ‘It is decidedly so’, ‘Without a doubt’, ‘Yes – definitely’, ‘You may rely on it’, ‘As I see it, yes’, ‘Most likely’, ‘Outlook good’, ‘Yes Signs point to yes’, ‘Reply hazy’, ’try again‘, ’Ask again later‘, ’Better not tell you now‘, ’Cannot predict now‘, ’Concentrate and ask again‘, ’Dont count on it‘, ’My reply is no‘, ’My sources say no‘, ’Aviral is great guy‘, ’Outlook not so
```

```
good‘, ’Very doubtful‘]
print(’ __ __ _____ _____ _____ ___ ‘)
print(’ | \/ | /\ / ____|_ _/ ____| / _ \ ‘)
print(’ | \ / | / \ | | __ | || | | (_) |‘)
print(’ | |\/| | / /\ \| | |_ | | || | > _ < ‘)
print(’ | | | |/ ____ \ |__| |_| || |____ | (_) |‘)
print(’ |_| |_/_/ \_\_____|_____\_____| \___/ ‘)
print(’‘)
print(’‘)
print(’‘)
print(’Hello the reader of Aviral Book, I am the Magic 8 Ball Fortune teller, can i get your name please?‘)
name = input()
print(’hello ‘ + name)
def Magic8Ball():
print(’Ask me a question.‘)
input()
print(answers[random.randint(0, len(answers) - 1)])
print(’I hope that helped!‘)
Replay()
def Replay():
print(’Do you have another question? [Y/N] ‘)
reply = input()
if reply == ’Y‘:
Magic8Ball()
elif reply == ’N‘:
exit()
else:
print(’I apologies, I did not catch that. Please repeat.')
Replay()
Magic8Ball()
```

Output:

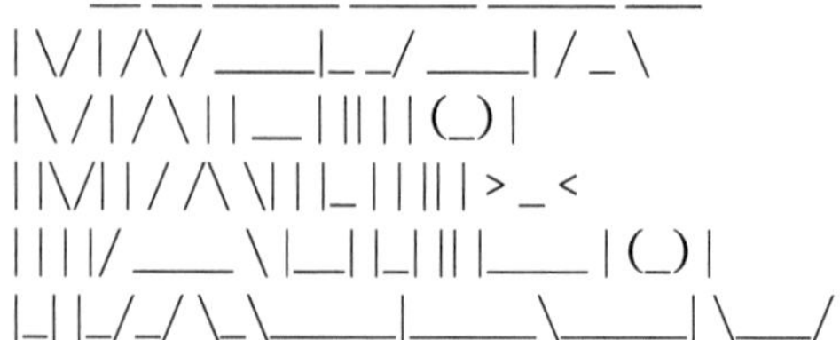

- Hello the reader of Aviral Book, I am the Magic 8 Ball Fortune teller, can i get your name please?

(Now i will enter my name, Aviral, then the output will be)

- hello Aviral
- Ask me a question.

(If we enter anything, it will display randomly answers from answers given by us)

(like if i entered at the time of writing this book, How is my day today? , the output it has given)

- As I see it, yes
- I hope that helped!
- Do you have another question? [Y/N]

(If i enter here, Y , it will show below output & game runs forever)

- Ask me a question.

Project - 4:

Create a Python project to roll a Dice Simulator.

Python Code:

```
import random
while True:
print(“' 1. roll the dice 2. exit “')
user = int(input("what you want to do\n"))
if user==1:
number = random.randint(1,6)
print(number)
else:
break
```

Output:

- 1. roll the dice 2. exit
- what you want to do

(If i enter, 1 , it will roll and answer randomly, & ask same ques again like below)

- 4
- 1. roll the dice 2. exit
- what you want to do

(if now i will enter, 2 , it will not show any output:)

Project - 5:

Create a Python project "Guess a number game".

Python Code:

```
import random
number = random.randint(1,10)
for i in range(0,3):
user = int(input("guess the number")) if user == number:
print("Hurray!!")
print(f"you guessed the number right it’s {number}")
break
if user != number:
print(f"Your guess is incorrect the number is {number}")
```

Output:

- guess the number

(suppose I enter 5)

- guess the number

(suppose I enter 6)

- guess the number

(suppose I enter 1)

- Your guess is incorrect the number is 8

Project - 6:

Create a Python project to generate random password from taking user input (Password length).

Python Code:

1. import random
2. passlen = int(input("enter the length of password"))
3. s="abcdefghijklmnopqrstuvwxyz01234567890

ABCDEFGHIJKLMNOPQRSTUVWXYZ!@#$%^&*()?"

1. p = "".join(random.sample(s,passlen))
2. print (p)

Output:

- enter the length of password

(suppose i enter 7, then the output will be)

- 5^GoMeY

Project - 7:

Create a Python project to binary search whether the number is present in the list or not.

Python Code:

```
lst = [1, 3, 2, 4, 5, 6, 9, 8, 7, 10]
lst.sort()
first = 0
last = len(lst) - 1
mid = (first + last) // 2
item = int(input("enter the number to be search"))
found = False
while (first <= last and not found):
mid = (first + last) // 2
if lst[mid] == item:
print(f"found at location {mid}")
found = True
else:
if item < lst[mid]:
last = mid - 1
else:
first = mid + 1
if found == False:
print("Number not found")
```

Output:

- enter the number to be search

    (If i will enter, 7 , then the output will be:)

- found at location 6

    (Now if we run it send time)

- enter the number to be search

    (suppose If i will enter, 11 , then the output will be:)

- Number not found

    (this is because, 11 is not present in the list)

Project - 8:

Create a Simple Calculator using Python.

Python Code:

```
num1 – input("First Number:\n")
operator = input("Operator (+, -, *, /):\n")
num2 = input("Second Number:\n")
num1 = float(num1)
num2 = float(num2)
out = None
if operator == "+":
out = num1 + num2
```

```
elif operator == "-":
out = num1 - num2
elif operator == "*":
out = num1 * num2
elif operator == "/":
out = num1 / num2
print("Answer: " + str(out))
```

Output:

- First Number:
- 2
- Operator (+, -, *, /):
- +
- Second Number:
- 5
- Answer: 7.0

Project - 9:

Create a Simple Calculator using Python which shows full calculation method.

Python Code:

```
def add(x, y):
return x + y
def subtract(x, y):
return x - y
```

```
def multiply(x, y):
return x * y
def divide(x, y):
return x / y print("Select operation.")
print("1.Add")
print("2.Subtract")
print("3.Multiply")
print("4.Divide")
while True:
choice = input("Enter choice(1/2/3/4): ")
if choice in (‘1’, ‘2’, ‘3’, ‘4’):
num1 = float(input("Enter first number: "))
num2 = float(input("Enter second number: "))
if choice == ‘1’:
print(num1, "+", num2, "=", add(num1, num2))
elif choice == ‘2’:
print(num1, "-", num2, "=", subtract(num1, num2))
elif choice == ‘3’:
print(num1, "*", num2, "=", multiply(num1, num2))
elif choice == ‘4’:
print(num1, "/", num2, "=", divide(num1, num2))
break
else:
print("Invalid Input")
```

Output:

- Select operation.
- 1.Add
- 2.Subtract
- 3.Multiply
- 4.Divide
- Enter choice(1/2/3/4): 2

- Enter first number: 3
- Enter second number: 3
- 3.0 - 3.0 = 0.0

Project - 10:

Create a Simple Project of Python to print table by taking user input:

```
n=int(input("Enter The Number : "))
i=1
while(i<=10):
t=n*i
print(n,"x",i,"=",t)
i=i+1
```

Output:

Enter The Number : 19

(suppose we have entered 19, to print 19 table, the output will be)

19 x 1 = 19

19 x 2 = 38

19 x 3 = 57

19 x 4 = 76

19 x 5 = 95

19 x 6 = 114

19 x 7 = 133

19 x 8 = 152

19 x 9 = 171
19 x 10 = 190

Happy Coding!

Printed by Libri Plureos GmbH in Hamburg,
Germany